GOD'S BEST TWO GIFTS

JOHN & GWEN FEEHAN

GOD'S BEST TWO GIFTS

By John & Gwen Feehan

Trade paperback ISBN: 978-1-60039-138-5

All Scripture quotations are taken from:
The Holy Bible, New King James Version
© 1984 by Thomas Nelson, Inc.

Cover and Interior Illustrations: Megan Marshall
Editing, Interior Design and Production: Brett Burner

GOD'S BEST TWO GIFTS

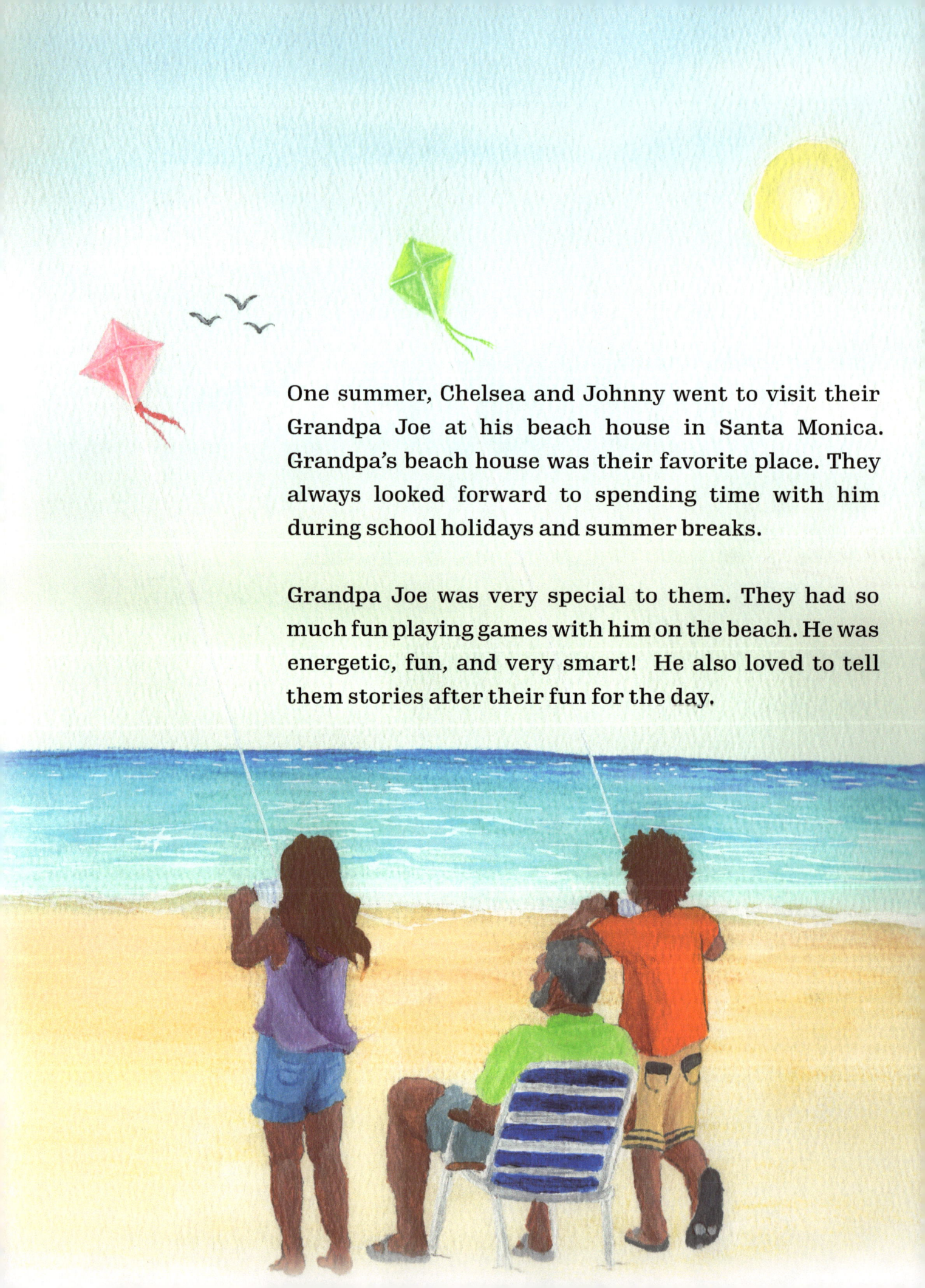

One summer, Chelsea and Johnny went to visit their Grandpa Joe at his beach house in Santa Monica. Grandpa's beach house was their favorite place. They always looked forward to spending time with him during school holidays and summer breaks.

Grandpa Joe was very special to them. They had so much fun playing games with him on the beach. He was energetic, fun, and very smart! He also loved to tell them stories after their fun for the day.

One day, after hours of flying kites on the beach, they went back to the house for a glass of lemonade and a plate full of cookies. Chelsea and Johnny sat on the front porch and watched the birds fly overhead as the waves crashed on the shore.

Grandpa gazed at the beauty of the sand and the sky and said, "Today, I want to share a great love story with you. You've already heard how God created all this beauty just for us, but I want you to know the whole story about God's love. I want you both to see how each of you has a part in the greatest love story ever told. Do you want to hear it?"

Chelsea and Johnny felt their hearts beating faster. Chelsea said, "Yes, please tell us, Grandpa!"

Johnny set down a half-eaten cookie. "Yes, please! We want to hear about it!"

Grandpa smiled at their eagerness. "This is the greatest love story ever told. I like to call it, 'God's Best Two Gifts.'"

Chelsea and Johnny looked at each other and smiled. They had a feeling this would be Grandpa's best story yet! Grandpa Joe leaned forward in his chair and began his story.

"It all starts with the history of God's Creation..."

THE HISTORY OF CREATION

In the beginning God created the heavens and the earth. His Spirit moved over the waters, and He said, "Let there be light." Then He called the light day and the darkness night. He created the sun, the moon, and the stars. He made dry land and the seas and caused all manner of plants to grow.

Then He created the sea creatures and every living creature on land and in the air, the animals, the birds, and every living creeping thing. And God said, "It is good!"

Within five days, God had created the heavens and earth and all the creatures that lived in it. Then God saw everything He made, and it was good.

God then planted a garden where every tree was beautiful and good for food. Then God said, "Let Us make man in Our likeness." And God formed a man out of the earth and breathed the breath of life into him. He was alive!

God blessed the man, Adam, with the authority over all of the earth.

Then God said, "It's not good for man to be alone." So He put Adam to sleep and made a woman from one of Adam's ribs. She was Adam's helper, and she was called "Eve."

God said to Adam and Eve, "Replenish the earth so that everything may multiply and be fruitful." He blessed these two who were most like Him. Mankind was His best creation of all!

God told them to take care of the garden. They could eat from any of the trees they wanted ... except one. God told them there was only one rule to follow. He commanded them, "Don't eat from the tree of the knowledge of good and evil in the middle of the garden. Because if you do, you will die."

When the evening and the morning of the sixth day had passed, God was done with his work. He looked at everything He had made in the first six days, and indeed it was *very* good!

On the seventh day, He rested from all of the work He had done.

ADAM AND EVE

Adam and Eve lived happily in the garden God had created. They ate from all the trees except for the one God told them not to eat from: the tree of the knowledge of good and evil.

But Satan, the devil, had a plan to trick them. One day he went to Eve in the form of a snake and said, "Did God really say you must not eat from the tree in the middle of the garden."

Eve said, "Yes, God said we would die."

Then Satan, speaking through the serpent, said, "Nothing bad will happen to you. You won't die, Eve! He knows that if you eat of it you will be like God! You will know all about good and evil!"

Eve liked that idea. And seeing that the fruit looked good, Eve took a bite of the fruit. She offered it to Adam who ate it too!

Satan's plan had worked! He had tricked them into disobeying God. And because they disobeyed God, Satan obtained all the authority that was given to Adam. Satan now had all power on earth!

Later that day, God came into the garden looking for Adam and Eve. He called out to them, "Where are you?"

Adam answered from behind a bush where they were hiding, "We are here. We were afraid and hid."

God asked, "Why are you afraid?"

"Because we realized we had no clothes on," Adam responded,

God said, "Who told you that you had no clothes on? Did you eat from the tree that I told you not to eat from?"

Adam said, "Yes, the woman gave it to me."

Eve said, "The snake fooled me. I ate it too."

God said to the snake, "I must punish you. You will crawl on your belly with your face in the dust!" He said to Satan, the serpent, "You are cursed, and there will be conflict between your children and Eve's children." God told Satan that He would bring someone into the world to *take back* the authority He had given Adam. By disobeying and sinning against God's Word, Adam had given over to Satan his authority and power over the earth.

Satan was evil and the father of lies. Satan didn't care what God had said. He had stolen Adam's authority. Satan was now the ruler of the world. If God sent someone to take his authority, Satan knew he would kill him.

The world was now in trouble.

Now God had to punish Adam and Eve for disobeying His word. He said to them, "You cannot live in the garden anymore." They left the garden, and angels were sent to guard the entrance.

God did not stop loving Adam and Eve. In fact, He already had a plan to save them from dying. His plan was a person: Jesus, God's only Son.

JESUS IS BORN

Many, many years later, God sent the angel Gabriel to the city of Nazareth in Galilee, where a young virgin girl named Mary lived. She was soon going to be married to Joseph, a descendant of King David. When Gabriel appeared to Mary, he told her she was going to have a baby!

"But how?" asked Mary. "I am not married yet."

The angel said, "the Spirit of God will do this, and put a special baby in you. He will be called Jesus, the Son of God!" Even though Mary did not understand, she agreed to do what God wanted.

Soon after, Mary hurried to visit Elizabeth, her relative, to tell her about the baby. Elizabeth was happy and surprised to see Mary. She told Mary that even though she was very old, she was going to have a baby too! He would be called John, and he would grow up to become John the Baptist. An angel had told her husband, Zacharias, a priest, that even though Elizabeth was old, "With God all things are possible."

The time came for Mary to deliver her baby. The Son of Man, Jesus, was born in a stable with cows and donkeys because there were no rooms available in town.

Angels appeared to shepherds out in the fields who were watching over their sheep and told them the good news: "The Messiah is born!" They saw a bright star over the stable, where they went to see and worship the baby Jesus. Wise men from far, far away also saw the star and knew that the King of the Jews had been born. They came on camels and brought gifts of gold, frankincense, and myrrh for Jesus.

JESUS'S MINISTRY

Jesus's cousin, John, known as John the Baptist, grew up and lived in the desert by the Jordon River. Many people would come to hear him preach. He declared that one greater than he would take away the sins of the world. He said, "Ask for the forgiveness of your sins and be baptized." Many people came to the Jordan River where he was baptizing. John told the people: "I baptize with water, but someone is coming who will baptize you with the Holy Spirit and fire."

He was talking about Jesus.

Jesus was thirty years old when He came to John to be baptized in the Jordan River. John protested, "Jesus, you are not a sinner. Why should you be baptized?" But Jesus told him it was what God wanted, so John baptized him.

As Jesus came out of the water, the heavens opened and he saw the Spirit of God—the Holy Spirit—coming down like a dove and alighting upon him! Suddenly, the voice of God came from heaven and said, "This is my beloved Son. I am well pleased with Him!"

After Jesus was baptized, the Holy Spirit led Jesus out into the wilderness. He did not eat for forty days and forty nights. Weak from not eating, Satan, the devil, came and tried to tempt Jesus into doing things He should not do. The devil tried to trick Him three times.

First, the devil challenged Him: "If you are the Son of God, command these stones to become bread so you can eat."

Next, the devil showed Jesus all the kingdoms of the world and said, "I have been given all authority over these kingdoms and can give it to whoever I wish. If you, Jesus will bow down and worship me, I will give it all to you."

Finally, Satan tempted Jesus to throw himself off the temple in view of everyone so the angels could save Him.

But Jesus denied the devil's every temptation saying, "Get behind me, Satan, for God's word says to worship God and serve God only!" So Satan left Him.

Then Jesus, filled with the power of the Spirit, departed from the wilderness to begin His three year ministry.

Jesus returned to Nazareth, his hometown, going into the synagogue and reading God's Word to the people there. "The Spirit of God is upon me. I will preach to the poor, free the captives, heal the hurting, and give sight to the blind." He told them He was sent by the Father to be the promised Messiah! The people and religious leaders were shocked and upset by His claims, and in anger they drove Him out to the edge of the city where they could throw Him over the cliff. But Jesus walked right through the crowd untouched, and left Nazareth.

Jesus then traveled the land choosing men who would follow Him. They were called disciples. Jesus and his disciples traveled throughout Israel, teaching and preaching about repentance from sin and the kingdom of God, healing the sick and giving sight to the blind. He told the bad spirits to get out of people. He even brought the dead back to life!

Because of his teaching and the many miracles He performed, Jesus was becoming very famous and well-loved among the people, but the religious leaders hated him. Afraid of losing their power over the people, they plotted to kill him.

After three years, it was now time for Jesus to go to Jerusalem and do what God, His Father, had sent Him to do.

There in Jerusalem, the night before Passover, an important Jewish holiday, Jesus went with his disciples to an upper room where they could eat the special Passover meal together. Jesus took and blessed the bread and wine, and He gave both to them saying, "This is my body and my blood which is given for you. Remember me."

He told them that one of them would betray Him. Then Judas, one of the disciples, slipped away from the table and left. Jesus knew that Judas had made a deal with the religious leaders to turn him in to them for money.

Jesus told his disciples that He was going to suffer great things, but that He was doing it for their sake. They didn't yet understand what He meant, but later they would.

After supper, Jesus and the disciples went to the garden of Gethsemane so Jesus could pray. He knew His time had come.

The religious leaders paid Judas thirty pieces of silver to lead the temple guards to Jesus. Judas told the guards, "The one I kiss is Jesus."

When they arrived at the garden, Judas went up to Jesus and kissed Him on the cheek. Jesus said to Judas, "Judas, you betray the Son of God with a kiss?" The guards then arrested Jesus.

The disciples then ran away in all directions, afraid for themselves.

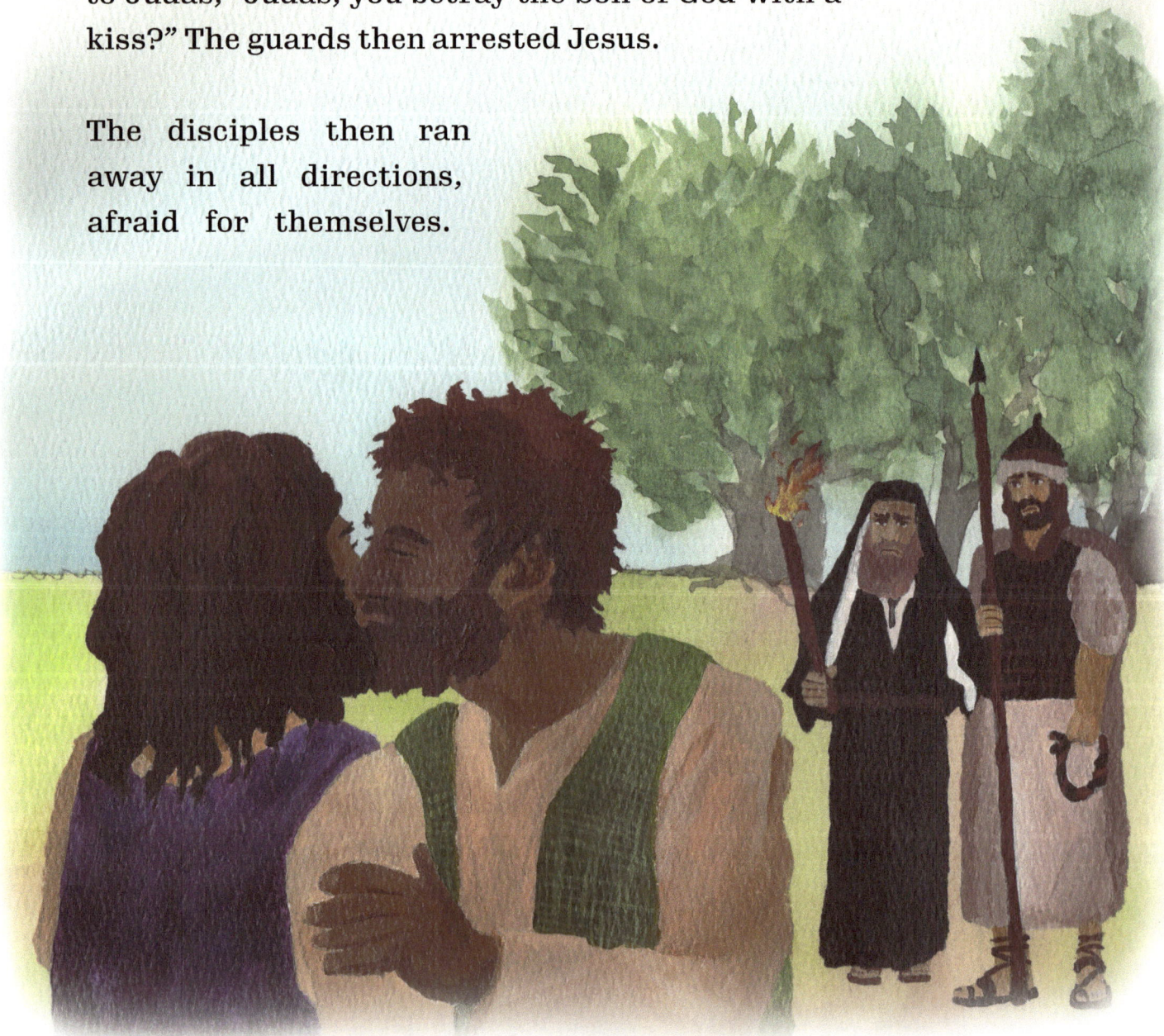

JESUS'S ARREST AND CRUCIFIXION

Jesus was taken to the religious leaders. They questioned Jesus and then asked Him if He claimed to be the Son of God, and Jesus said: "I am." But the religious leaders did not believe Him and said He blasphemed God. They declared that because He said this, according to Jewish law He should be put to death.

But the Romans, who ruled over the Jews at that time, had a law that Jews were not allowed to put people to death. Because of this law, the religious leaders sent Jesus to Pontius Pilate, the Roman Ruler of Judea, so the Romans could kill Him.

So Jesus was taken to Pontius Pilate. Pilate asked Jesus many questions, but Jesus did not answer him. Finally, he asked Jesus, "Are you who you say you are, King of the Jews?"

Jesus responded, "Yes, I am what you say!" Pilate took Jesus back to the people and religious leaders and said, "This man has done nothing wrong. He should not die."

But the people shouted, "Crucify him!'

Pilate didn't want to put Jesus to death, so he chose to have Jesus whipped severely. Pilate then brought Jesus back, badly beaten, and said to the people, "See I have punished Him."

Pilate then said, "At Passover I have agreed to release one prisoner to you. Do you want Barabbas, a thief and murderer, or Jesus, King of the Jews?"

All the people and religious leaders yelled out, "Release Barabbas!"

Pilate asked, "What should I do with Jesus?"

The religious leaders and the crowd shouted, "Crucify Him!"

Pilate had no choice. Jesus was sentenced, and led away to his death.

The soldiers made a crown of thorns and jammed it onto Jesus's head declaring, "Hail, King of the Jews." They made Jesus carry a wooden cross through the streets of Jerusalem to a hill outside the city called Golgotha.

Then the Roman soldiers nailed Jesus's hands and feet to the cross. Two thieves were also crucified with Him, one on each side of Him.

A sign was made for the top of the cross which read, "Jesus of Nazareth, King of the Jews."

Jesus's mother, Mary, and his disciple John, stood at the foot of the cross. Jesus asked them to look after one another. In great pain, Jesus asked God to forgive the people who had done all this to him, "For they do not know what they do!"

The sky turned dark, and for three hours the land was as dark as night! Then Jesus gave out a loud cry saying, "It is finished, Father! I give up my spirit to you." He took His last breath and died. At that moment, the ground shook! One of the soldiers there who saw and heard all of this said, "Truly this man was the Son of God!"

Because it was Passover, the religious leaders didn't want Jesus left on the cross. Jesus's friends gently took His body down from the cross and laid him in a tomb.

Then they rolled a huge stone across the opening of the tomb.

The next day, Jesus's family and friends hid from the religious leaders, crying because Jesus had died.

On Sunday morning, the third day after Jesus died, Mary Magdalene and some other women went to visit his tomb. They found the stone had been rolled back and Jesus body was gone! They burst into tears, believing His body had been stolen. They then saw an angel of the Lord who said to them, "Why are you seeking the living among the dead? Jesus is not here, He is risen!"

JESUS IS RISEN!

Then Mary saw a man who she thought was the gardener. She asked him, "Do you know where they have taken my master?"

He said to her, "Mary," and she knew it was Jesus's voice! Jesus *had* risen from the dead! Mary was in wonder and amazement. Jesus told her to go back and tell the others that He was alive.

Concerned that people would believe that Jesus was risen, the guards and the chief priests spread a lie that Jesus body had been stolen from the tomb by the disciples, and many Jews believed this lie! But over five hundred people would see Jesus alive before He ascended to His Father God in heaven!

Later that night, as the disciples were gathered together in a room in Jerusalem, Jesus suddenly appeared and stood saying, "Peace to you!" They were all terrified and frightened thinking they were looking at a spirit, but Jesus said, "See and feel the holes in my hands and feet, it is Me."

Jesus then asked for food and ate it! He showed them the Scriptures written hundreds of years before by the prophets. They told of His coming, and about how, when, and where He would be born. He explained to them it was foretold that the Christ would suffer a beating, die, and rise from the dead on the third day.

Jesus directed His disciples to preach in His name, so that all nations would hear about God's *first gift* for all mankind: Jesus himself!

The disciples became apostles, and they and the men and women who followed Jesus went out all over the land telling many people about Jesus and how much God loved them. They taught how Jesus was sent to die for their sins and came back to life again on the third day, that Jesus defeated death and took back the authority Adam had given to Satan. They preached that those who believed Jesus died and rose again, repented, and asked for forgiveness of their sins, would be forgiven and live with Him forever in heaven.

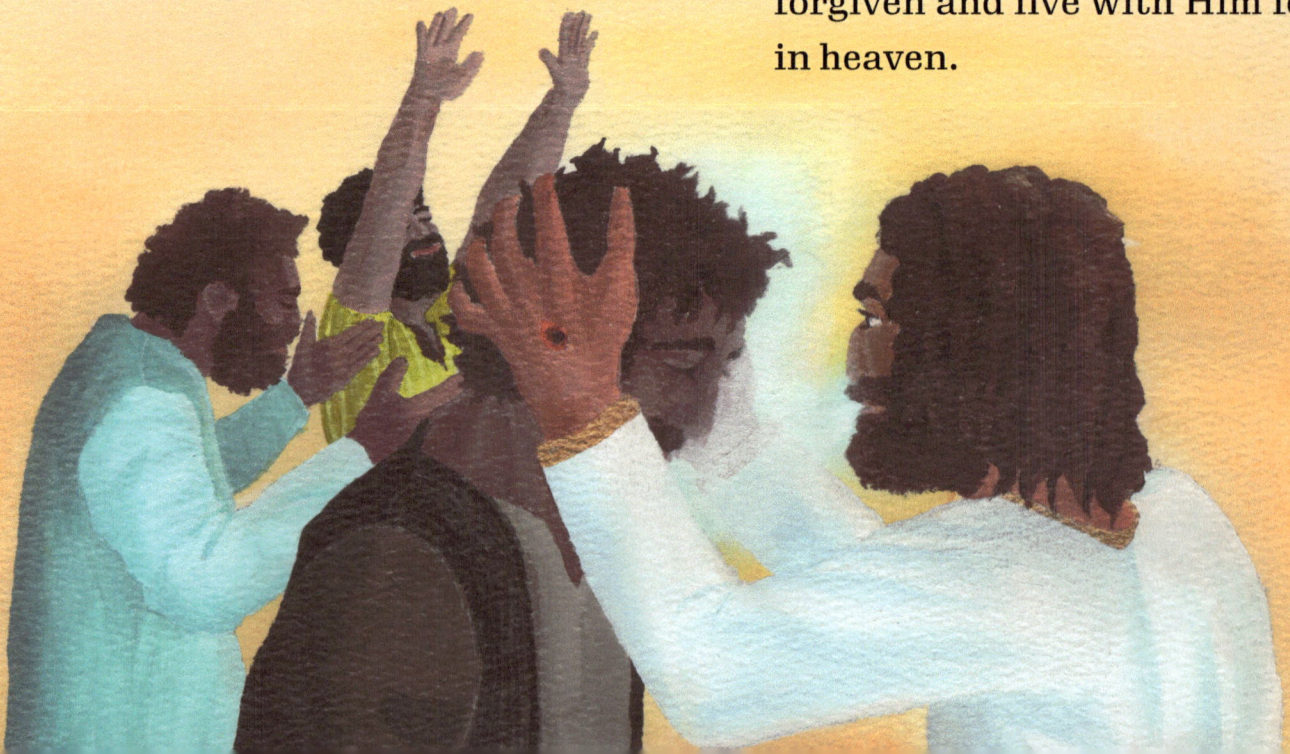

THE FIRST GIFT

"Salvation in Jesus Christ is the *first gift* from God the Father!" said Grandpa.

"That's an amazing story, Grandpa!" Johnny said. Chelsea reached out and grabbed Grandpa's hand. "Grandpa, I want the gift. How do we get it?"

Grandpa smiled. "If you believe Jesus is the Son of God, and that He died for your sins and is alive in heaven even now, and if you want to receive the free gift of eternal life and live forever with Jesus Christ in heaven with the Father, then all you have to do is say this simple prayer to receive Him:

"Father, I know that I have done some bad things. I'm sorry. Forgive me.

"Father, I thank you that you said you would forgive me when I asked.

"I know you gave your Son, Jesus, to die for me! I believe He rose again on the third day and is alive with you in heaven today. And Jesus, I ask you to come into my life and be the Lord of my Life.

"I give you my life, Jesus. I thank you that I am now a child of God and I will spend forever in heaven with you. AMEN."

"Amen!" chimed the children together.

Grandpa smiled. "I'm so happy for you both! But now ... I want to tell you about God's *second* gift!"

"There's more?" asked Chelsea.

"There's *more!*" said Grandpa.

GOD'S SECOND GIFT

On the night Jesus was arrested, while Jesus was still with his followers having supper in the upper room, He had told them He would go soon to be with His Father in heaven. But He promised to send to them the Helper, the promise of the Father, who is the Holy Spirit.

"The Holy Spirit," Jesus said, "will comfort you, lead you, teach you, and remind you of all I have said."

The Holy Spirit is God's *second* gift for his followers.

After Jesus had risen and revealed Himself to His disciples, He breathed on them and said, "Receive the Holy Spirit."

One day, Jesus led his disciples out to Bethany, near the city. He commanded them to remain in Jerusalem until they received the power of the Holy Spirit!

He told them: "You shall receive power when the Holy Spirit has come upon you, and you will be my witnesses in Jerusalem, and in all Judea and Samaria, and to the ends of the earth."

While they watched, Jesus ascended into heaven. Then His followers went back to Jerusalem, happy and excited, waiting to be baptized with the Holy Spirit.

At that time, the Feast of the First Fruits, a Jewish holiday, was in Jerusalem. Jews and people from every country under heaven came. One special day, the disciples, Mary, the mother of Jesus, and 120 more people were there in the upper room.

Suddenly, there came a sound from heaven, like a rushing mighty wind, filling the whole house, and tongues as of fire settled on each of them!

They were all baptized with the power of the Holy Spirit, and then they began to speak as the Spirit gave them words!

There were devout Jews from every nation living in Jerusalem at that time. When they heard the sound, they came to where the apostles were. The apostles went out to the people, and as they spoke, the crowd marveled, saying, "Aren't all these people who are speaking Galileans? But we hear them speaking about the wonderful works of God in our own language!"

Then the Apostle Peter spoke up and told the crowd about how the prophets of God had written and prophesied about the death and resurrection of Jesus, the Christ! He told them to repent of their sin and be baptized, and they would receive the Holy Spirit too!

That day, three thousand people believed them. They received Jesus as their Lord and Savior! God really loved them and sent Jesus to save them from eternal death!

The church of Jesus Christ had begun!

The Apostles began to teach about Jesus in Jerusalem, then throughout Judea, and even into Samaria, and people began to believe all throughout the land!

There was a man named Saul, a religious leader known as a Pharisee, who hated Jesus and had His followers thrown in prison or put to death. One day Saul was riding to Damascus to arrest some of the followers of Jesus. All of a sudden, a bright light from heaven shone down on Saul and knocked him to the ground. He then heard a voice from heaven saying, "Saul, Saul, why are you persecuting me?" Saul said, "Who are you lord?" And the voice said, "I am Jesus."

After that, Saul became a believer of Jesus too! He changed his name to Paul, and God sent him to many nations to preach the good news of Jesus. He planted many churches, and even more people believed and received God's only Son, Jesus, as their Lord and Savior! Paul taught that Jesus baptizes us in the Holy Spirit. This was a promise from our heavenly Father so we can go out and tell others about Jesus.

Followers of Jesus have been telling His love story for over two thousand years—and still do to this day!

God wants to send you too!

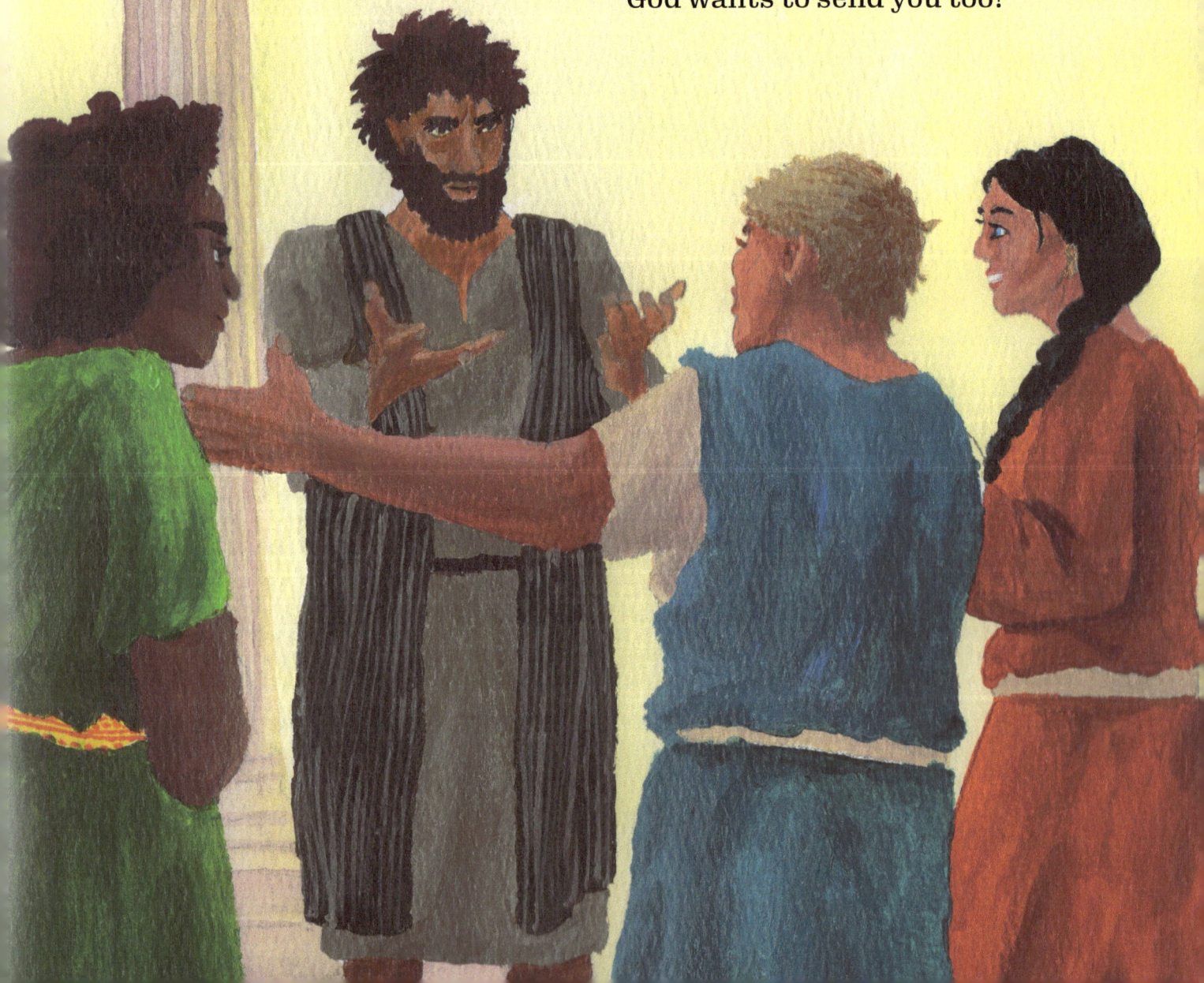

RECEIVING THE SECOND GIFT

These are God's best two gifts: JESUS and THE HOLY SPIRIT.

John the Baptist said, "I baptize with water, but Jesus baptizes with the Holy Spirit and fire."

Jesus is the baptizer. When you receive Jesus as your Lord and Savior, the Holy Spirit comes to live inside of you. Think of it like a "guest room." He wants to be your best friend. He wants to guide you, to comfort you, to give you joy and happiness, and give you good gifts!

After His resurrection, Jesus had breathed on his disciples and told them to receive the Holy Spirit. The disciples were the first believers. And still today, when a person has received Jesus as their Savior, they too receive the Holy Spirit.

And just as He wanted the disciples to receive and experience the power of the Holy Spirit, He wants you to receive this power too. This is called the baptism of the Holy Spirit! It is a gift from the Father.

One of the gifts of the Holy Spirit is called the *gift of tongues*. He uses your mouth to talk to God, and He gives you a prayer language that no one understands except God and Jesus. He prays perfect prayers for you, even when you don't know how to pray!

The Holy Spirit is gentle, He doesn't want to overpower you! He wants to give you power and even help you understand the things of God better. He wants to be your best friend. All He asks is to use your mouth and tongue to speak out loud.

The Holy Spirit wants to lead you into the gifts and desires God has for your life. Would you like to invite Him to come out of your "guest room" and receive His second gift for you?

It all begins with a simple prayer. When you finish, close your eyes and just start moving your mouth. The Holy Spirit will come up from your guestroom and do the rest. He doesn't come from your mind, so it won't happen by thinking about it. You may not understand what He is saying—no one else will either, that's all right. *God understands.* That's all that matters. Just trust Him! It doesn't matter if one word comes out or many, don't stop.

Now lift up your arms and say this prayer:

"Holy Spirit, I know you're inside me, in my "guest room." I ask you to lead me and guide me and pray for me to my heavenly Father. Holy Spirit, I ask you to take over my body from the top of my head to the soles of my feet. I give you my mouth and tongue. Holy Spirit, fill me now with joy, happiness, and peace. Give me my heavenly language. Baptize me now with your Spirit, power, and fire!"

Now take three deep breaths and start moving your mouth!

Pray in the Spirit every day. It's like using your muscles.
The more you use them the stronger you get!

Do you know what your gifts are?
Do you know your purpose in life?

God says, "Before I formed you, I knew you!" All the stages of your life were prepared before you even lived one day! God knew your gifts and your purpose because He is the One who wrote them in your own book. You are a part of God's love story. You are loved by God, and you are one of a kind!

We all have books in heaven.

Some day we will stand alone in front of God and he will ask us what we did with the gifts he gave us, and we will tell Him the story of our lives. We can't go to heaven and read our books but the Holy Spirit can.

Ask the Holy Spirit to show you how to use your gifts and walk out the plan God has for your life.

In that day when you stand before him, he will ask you what you did with your life and your gifts, and you can answer that you gave and shared your gifts to all. And then He will then say to you:

''Well done, good and faithful one! Welcome to heaven!"

God's Best Two Gifts are for you!

As Grandpa finished, Johnny said, "I want to experience the Holy Spirit like the disciples did!"

"Me too!" echoed Chelsea. Grandpa couldn't contain his smile! The sun was setting, and the beach was getting chilly. Grandpa said, "Let's go inside and I'll start a nice fire in the fireplace."

Before he could stand, Johnny got up and gave him a big hug. "Thank you, Grandpa!"

Then Chelsea hugged them both. "We love you, Grandpa!"

It was the best day of their lives. They were filled with so much joy and peace, and they knew their lives would never be the same. The whole world looked different. They'd had fun in the sun, but best of all, Chelsea and Johnny had decided to receive God's best two gifts, and they wanted to be part of God's love story and be His chosen ones forever!

God's greatest gift was Jesus Christ, His only Son. He came down from heaven to earth and died for us to take away our sin so that we can live forever with Him!

His second greatest gift, the gift of the Holy Spirit, was given after Jesus went up to heaven. The Holy Spirit works through us to give us the Father's heart and mind to do great things for Him, in Jesus name. The Holy Spirit gives us the power we need to show Jesus to our world.

Won't you receive them too?

"Taste and see that the Lord is good!
Blessed is the one who trusts in Him!"
(Psalm 34:8)

SCRIPTURE INDEX

Follow along in the story with these Bible references:

www.ingramcontent.com/pod-product-compliance
Lightning Source LLC
Chambersburg PA
CBHW061050090426

42740CB00002B/97